This book belongs to

_____

Neil Armstrong

By Mary Nhin

This book is dedicated to my children - Mikey, Kobe, and Jojo.

Copyright © 2023 by Grow Grit Press LLC. All rights reserved. No part of this book may be reproduced in any form without permission in writing from the publisher. Please send bulk order requests to growgritpress@gmail.com
Paperback ISBN: 978-1-63731-685-6 Hardcover ISBN: 978-1-63731-687-0
Printed and bound in the USA. MiniMovers.tv

I was born on August 5th, 1930 in Ohio. When I was young, my father took me to air shows and aviation exhibitions. I even got to ride on a plane when I was 6 years old. This helped grow my fascination with flying and exploring the unknown.

I loved flying so much that I received my flying certificate at age 16 before I even received my license to drive a car.

I faced many challenges in my life. When I was a Navy Pilot during the Korean War, while flying around hills in enemy territory, I lost 2 feet on the right wing of my plane when I ran into a trap.

I stayed calm and tried to fly back to friendly territory the best I could. I made the decision to eject myself from the plane and used my parachute. Fortunately, I was rescued by a fellow soldier.

After I served in the Korean War as a pilot, I went to Purdue University where I studied aeronautical engineering while I took flight lessons.

After graduation in 1962, I became a test pilot for the National Advisory Committee for Aeronautics (NACA), which later became known as NASA.

In 1966, I was the first civilian astronaut to fly into space as the commander of the Gemini 8. The mission was aborted when the thruster got stuck.

I trained and learned from the mistakes that had been made. Over time, I became a capsule communicator where I talked to rookies on missions and gave guidance from the ground.

In 1966, I was back as commander for Gemini 11. This time, I knew the systems better than before.

Finally, my mission to go to the moon had come.
It was me, Michael Collins, and Buzz Aldrin.

I was nervous when our landing didn't go as planned. I used my flight skills to avoid any harm from the craters near us and in a timely manner to reduce fuel waste.

After walking out onto the moon's surface, I planted the American flag into the ground. It was very cool to be the first man to step onto the moon's surface.

While there, my crew and I spent over 22 hours exploring the moon's surface.

When we tried to leave and go back home, we noticed that the ignition switch was broken. Fortunately, we found a pen to reach and push the circuit breaker to start the launch.

We successfully landed the spacecraft to Earth by landing it in the Pacific Ocean. Shortly after, we were picked up by the USS Hornet and kept in a capsule to quarantine for 18 days.

To celebrate the success of our mission, a parade was held in New York and Chicago.

I decided after this that I would never fly to space again, as I had met my goal and I was ready to explore other paths in my life.

I became a professor at the University of Cincinnati where I taught in the Department of Aerospace Engineering.

I was a strong advocate for space exploration and investigated failed missions. I was appointed to a commission by President Reagan to develop a plan to improve the American spaceflight in the 21st century.

When I passed away, many of my papers were donated to the University I taught at.

My legacy carries on even today, and in my hometown of Wapakoneta, you can visit the museum named after me to see all of my life journey.

Timeline

1930 - Neil is born

1946 - Neil receives flying certificate

1962 - Neil becomes pilot for NASA

1966 - Neil completes first space flight

1969 - Neil lands on the moon

minimovers.tv

 @marynhin   @GrowGrit
#minimoversandshakers

 Mary Nhin   Ninja Life Hacks

 Ninja Life Hacks

 @ninjalifehacks.tv

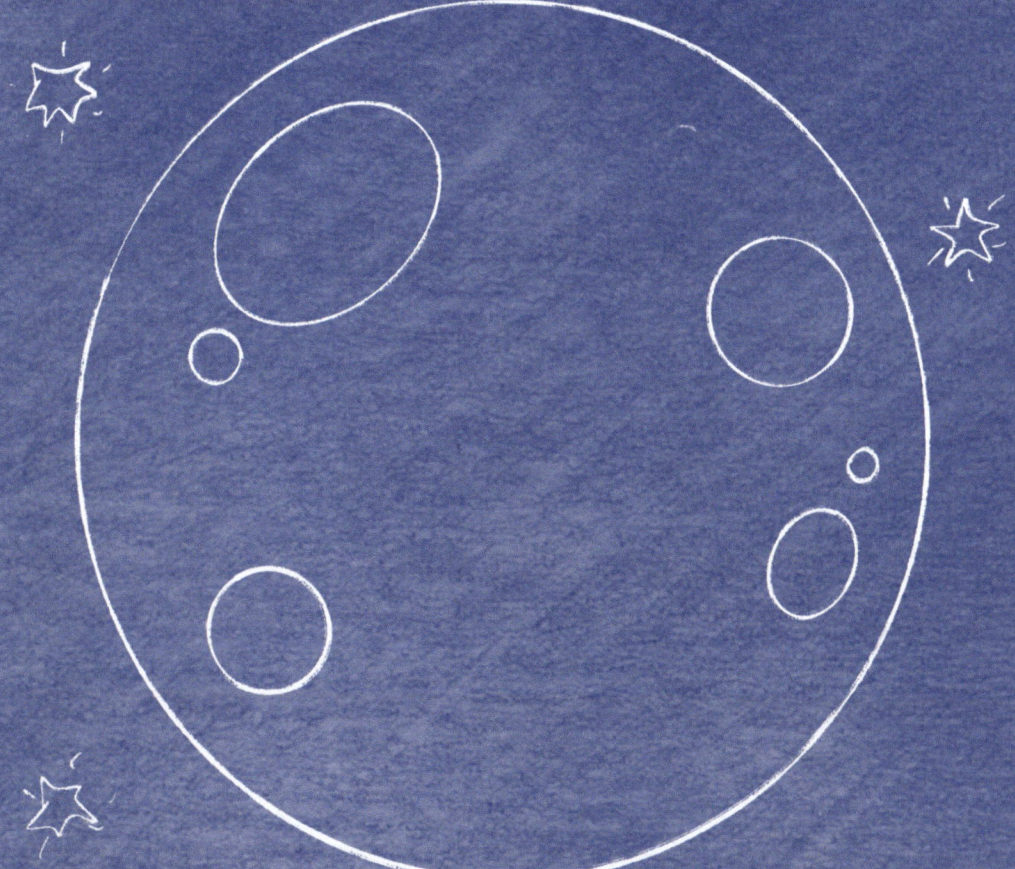

www.ingramcontent.com/pod-product-compliance
Lightning Source LLC
Chambersburg PA
CBHW041523070526
44585CB00002B/59